EXPLORING THE SCIENCE OF NATURE

The Nature and Science of
WINTER

Jane Burton and Kim Taylor

Gareth Stevens Publishing
MILWAUKEE

For a free color catalog describing Gareth Stevens Publishing's list of high-quality books and multimedia programs, call 1-800-542-2595 (USA) or 1-800-461-9120 (Canada). Gareth Stevens Publishing's Fax: (414) 225-0377.

Library of Congress Cataloging-in-Publication Data

Burton, Jane.
The nature and science of winter / by Jane Burton and Kim Taylor.
p. cm. — (Exploring the science of nature)
Includes bibliographical references and index.
Summary: Explains why the season of winter happens and how it
manifests itself in the weather and changes in plants and animals.
ISBN 0-8368-2191-2 (lib. bdg.)
1. Winter—Juvenile literature. [1. Winter.] I. Taylor, Kim.
II. Title. III. Series: Burton, Jane.
Exploring the science of nature.
QB637.8.B84 1999
508.2—dc21   99-14718

First published in North America in 1999 by
Gareth Stevens Publishing
1555 North RiverCenter Drive, Suite 201
Milwaukee, Wisconsin 53212 USA

This U.S. edition © 1999 by Gareth Stevens, Inc. Created with original © 1999 by
White Cottage Children's Books. Text © 1999 by Kim Taylor. Photographs © 1999 by
Jane Burton, Kim Taylor, and Mark Taylor. The photographs on pages 11 (*left*), 17 (*below*),
and 18 (*below*) are by Jan Taylor. The photographs on pages 15 (*top and left*) and 27 (*above*)
are by Robert Burton. Conceived, designed, and produced by White Cottage
Children's Books, 29 Lancaster Park, Richmond, Surrey TW10 6AB, England.
Additional end matter © 1999 by Gareth Stevens, Inc.

The rights of Jane Burton and Kim Taylor to be identified as the authors of this work
have been asserted by them in accordance with the Copyright, Design and Patents
Act 1988. Educational consultant, Jane Weaver; scientific adviser, Dr. Jan Taylor.

Printed in the United States of America

1 2 3 4 5 6 7 8 9 03 02 01 00 99

Contents

Words that appear in the glossary are printed in **boldface** type the first time they occur in the text.

The Meaning of Winter

The **axis** on which Earth spins is tilted at an angle of 23 degrees. As Earth travels around the Sun, its axis first leans toward the Sun and then leans away from it. Winter is the time when the axis leans away from the Sun.

The winter Sun never rises very high in the sky. The shortest day of the year in the Northern **Hemisphere** is December 21 or 22 — known as the winter **solstice**. However, in the Southern Hemisphere, the winter solstice is June 20 or 21.

The shortest day is not necessarily the coldest. Temperatures get continuously colder after the solstice, even though the days are growing longer and the Sun is rising higher. This is because large amounts of water take a long time to cool. Lakes and oceans still hold some of the warmth from the sunny days of summer and autumn. Not until they have lost this warmth does the air become bitter.

For many animals, winter means hunger and fear. It may be a hard time for plants, as well. They need water and light to grow, but all the water may be frozen, and the days may be short and dark. Our ancestors who lived in cold parts of the world must have also feared winter. They found shelter in caves. If they did not store a large amount of food in autumn, they probably did not survive the winter.

Top: Ivy berries turn from green to black as they ripen during the winter months.

Opposite: Red foxes play in a white fairyland of snow-covered trees.

Below: Fresh-fallen snow settles on the ripe berries of a cotoneaster bush.

A White Blanket

People who live in very cold climates know all about snow. After snow falls there, it lies over the ground all winter. In many parts of the world, snow is unknown because the climate is too warm. People who live in warm countries may have only seen pictures of snow or glimpsed it on the white caps of distant mountains. They find it difficult to believe that water can become a fine, white powder, so cold that it would make their fingers ache to touch it.

The reason snow is powdery is because it is made up of tiny **crystals**. These snow crystals form in clouds in the same way that raindrops form. When it rains, water **vapor** in the air **condenses**, forming droplets that gradually become bigger until they fall.

Right: The white cap on Mount Kilimanjaro is the only snow that this giraffe in eastern Africa will ever see.

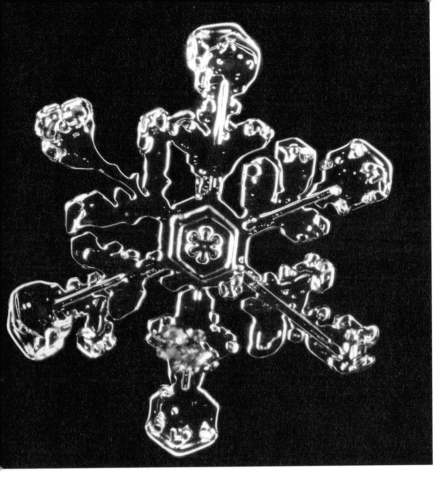

Left: A greatly magnified image of a melting snow crystal shows its six-sided shape.

Below: Animal tracks are readily visible in the Canadian snow. Much of Canada is covered in deep snow each winter.

If the air is cold enough, water vapor condenses directly into ice crystals that attract each other to form **snowflakes**. Amazingly, a large snowflake can be made up of thousands of crystals. The crystals are sometimes needle-shaped and sometimes six-sided. Occasionally, snow crystals fall separately without clumping together into flakes. Then it is easy to see their beautiful, star-like shapes.

The shape of snow crystals is based on the shape of water **molecules**. When a crystal forms from vapor, it builds up in layers, molecule by molecule. The molecules of water neatly stack together in a six-sided arrangement, producing tiny, glittering stars of ice.

Snow is not always powdery. Sometimes it is very sticky. It sticks to the branches of trees. It piles up on any type of surface, even on steep slopes. A silent, overnight fall of sticky snow can change a drab winter wood into a fairyland. Every rock, plant, and tiny twig carries its own glistening white cap of snow.

Right: Snow piles up in thick mounds on boulders in a stream.

Snow becomes sticky when the air temperature is just above the freezing point. The crystals in the snowflakes start to melt as the snowflakes fall. Each crystal is surrounded by a thin layer of water. Where the crystals touch, the water layers join. **Surface tension** in the water holds the crystals together and makes one snowflake stick to another, wherever they land. A sharp frost after a fall of sticky snow freezes the water, locking the crystals together. This creates a crunchy layer on top of the snow.

A snowfall can act like a blanket, keeping the ground underneath it from freezing. This is because air is trapped between snow crystals, and air is a good **insulator**. In fact, about nine-tenths of fresh snow is air. Only one-tenth is ice. Warmth from the Sun can penetrate through a layer of snow to warm the ground beneath it. In some northern countries, more life goes on *underneath* the snow than on top of it.

Below: Moles need to eat all year through. In winter, they continue to search their tunnels for worms, regardless of the cold weather above the ground.

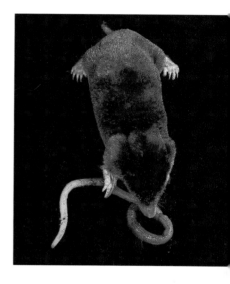

Left: A blanket of snow can keep the ground from freezing. Moles keep busy under the ground, pushing up mounds of unfrozen soil through the snow.

Coated with Crystals

Top: The edges and hairs on a bramble leaf sprout a growth of white crystals.

Above: Frost crystals on a spider's web make it look as though it were made of white string.

Right: A thin coat of frost covers mosses and ferns growing on the trunk of a big leaf maple.

One of the most beautiful scenes of winter in cold countries is the glinting layer of white frost crystals that sometimes covers everything. Needle-shaped crystals sprout from the edges of every leaf, every twig, and even from the strands of spiders' webs. When the Sun shines on a **hoarfrost** like this, a magical, glittering scene comes to life.

Frost can form only when the air close to the ground is moist. Water molecules in the cold air settle on solid objects and form crystals. Layers of ice, one molecule thick, build up, and the crystals grow. Rough surfaces attract frost more than smooth surfaces. Any little bristles on leaves, for instance, collect especially fine growths of frost.

Frost forms from clear, moist air. When the air is foggy and the temperature drops below freezing, droplets of water from the fog settle on solid objects and then freeze. This creates a layer of white **rime** in which ice crystals are not obvious.

Occasionally, fine rain falls during freezing conditions at ground level. Then, the rain forms a layer of clear ice on surfaces. Freezing rain can build up more than 0.4 inch (1 centimeter) thick. It can enclose every object in a jacket of glassy ice. Even big trees and electric lines sometimes collapse under the weight of ice.

Below: The air just above a frozen lake is very moist. Giant frost crystals grow and cover plants near the water, such as this reed.

Left: After a freezing rain, the stems and berries of a rose bush become encased in a thick layer of clear ice.

11

Top: Water on a lake in early winter soon freezes enough to bear the weight of a coot.

Above: Underground water freezes if it meets the ice-cold air of winter. Here, ground water trickling down a bank has frozen into magnificent icicles.

Right: Not all the water running down the outside of an icicle freezes onto it. Some water drips off the tip, forming an upward-growing mound of ice.

Just about everybody has seen ice as it comes out of a refrigerator, but only people living in cold regions have seen lakes freeze until the ice is 1.5 feet (0.5 meter) thick. Only in cold regions or high in the mountains do waterfalls freeze into domes and columns of solid ice.

Pure water turns from a liquid into a solid at 32° Fahrenheit (0° Celsius). A pond does not suddenly freeze over as soon as the air temperature drops to the freezing point, however. Instead, a network of spear-shaped crystals gradually grows over the surface of the water until a continuous layer of ice forms.

As more water freezes beneath the surface, the ice thickens. The freezing process is slow because water does not turn to ice as soon as temperatures reach the freezing point. Water has to release what is called its **latent heat** before it starts to turn to ice.

It seems unlikely, but waterfalls can freeze. Icicles several feet (meters) long can form in waterfalls during the freezing temperatures of winter. Incredible ice formations also build up where water splashes around a waterfall. The formations look like clear beads of glass, in many sizes, heaped among the rocks at the bottom of the waterfall.

Above: Ice that formed on the surface of this pond started out as spear-shaped crystals. Slow, gradual freezing caused long spears to form. When freezing is rapid, there is no time for big crystals to grow, and the ice is made up of tiny crystals.

Right: Because of the movement of their swimming, two swans keep a small patch of water open on an otherwise frozen lake.

Most liquids **contract** steadily as they cool, but water is different. It contracts until it reaches 39°F (4°C), and then it starts to **expand**. As the surface of a pond cools on a freezing winter's night, the cold water sinks to the bottom until the entire pond reaches 39°F (4°C). After this, only the surface layer gets colder and starts to freeze. This peculiar property of water is very important for fish and other animals that live in ponds and lakes. They stay at the bottom of the body of water, where the water temperature is survivable.

Seawater contains salt, and salt lowers the freezing point of water. The temperature of seawater can, therefore, be several degrees below freezing before ice starts to form. Thick layers of sea ice *do* form during winter in **polar regions**.

Below: Crucian carp rest at the bottom of some lakes in winter, where the water temperature is survivable at 39°F (4°C).

Air-breathing seals live under the ice, but they come to the surface to breathe. They chew at the edges of their breathing holes to keep the holes from icing over.

Large numbers of fish and **plankton** live in the cold polar water. The cold does not greatly affect these creatures because the water temperature below the surface layers does not vary much from one season to another.

Because the days are so short and lacking in light, however, green-plant plankton become scarce. This means there is no food for shrimps and other animals that eat the tiny, green-plant plankton. These animals then sink into deeper water to await spring.

Top: Adélie penguins are well adapted to the icy conditions of the Antarctic.

Left: Weddell seals in the Antarctic rest on an ice floe. While it is winter in the Northern Hemisphere, it is summer in the Southern Hemisphere.

Dormant Buds

Top: A nasturtium leaf before the first frost of winter is firm and round.

Above: Frost makes the cells in nasturtium leaves burst. When the frost melts, the leaves wither.

Right: The leaves of the poplar trees in the foreground will fall off before winter sets in. The leaves of the evergreen fir trees in the background can withstand frost.

When water turns to ice, it expands. That is why water pipes in a house sometimes burst when they freeze. If the water in a living thing, such as a leaf, freezes, the ice crystals that form inside its **cells** may burst, too. When cells burst, they die. A delicate leaf covered in frost will collapse once the frost melts because its cells have burst.

In cold climates, many types of plants shed their leaves before winter sets in. The trees that shed their leaves in autumn are called **deciduous**. The trees that keep their leaves throughout the year are called **evergreens**.

In parts of southern Africa and Australia, the winters are not very cold, but they are dry. Deciduous trees, such as baobabs, shed their leaves to avoid the effects of the coming drought, rather than the cold.

Left: The tightly packed leaves inside these oak buds contain very little water, and so are not damaged by frost.

Below: A baobab tree in Australia sheds its leaves — not because of the cold, but due to dryness.

When the leaves of deciduous trees fall, they leave behind hard, scaly buds on every twig. The buds contain many tiny new leaves, closely folded. These tightly packed leaves contain much less water than open leaves. For this reason, they are not damaged by frost. Each little package of new leaves remains **dormant** over winter.

Evergreen leaves are generally much tougher than deciduous leaves, and they hold less water. In fact, the water in some kinds of evergreen leaves contains chemicals that work like the anti-freeze mixtures used in car radiators. The natural anti-freeze in pine needles and holly leaves, for instance, keeps them from being damaged, even by a severe frost.

Left: The tough, evergreen leaves of holly withstand hard frost.

17

Winter Flowers

Top: The yellow flowers of gorse can be found at any time of year.

Below: White snowdrops push up through the snow even in mid-winter.

Below: In some parts of Australia, carpets of flowers open in winter. Winter is the only time there is enough rain for plants to grow.

In Mediterranean climates, many flowers open in winter. In winter, the weather there is cool and moist. By flowering in winter, plants avoid the scorching, dry heat of summer. Many plants in **arid** areas of Australia also flower during winter because that is the only time rain falls.

In colder climates, where there are severe frosts and the ground is often covered in snow, only a few specialized plants flower in winter. Plants called snowdrops and aconites push up through the snow to open their flowers in the winter sunshine.

Warmth from the Sun penetrates the snow and thaws the ground below. Energy from the Sun causes the flowers to grow. By flowering in winter, these plants do not have to compete with other flowers that open later in the year. In addition, any passing insect is guaranteed to be attracted to them for pollination.

Left: Winter aconites sense the warmth of the Sun penetrating the snow. They push their yellow flowers up through the snow.

Below: A delicate glacier lily breaks through the snow layer to open its flower.

Winter flowers also have the advantage of not being shaded by trees that burst into leaf in spring. Winter flowers are not smothered by the many other plants that grow later in the year.

Some plants produce flowers throughout the year. During any month — even the coldest — a few yellow flowers can be found on gorse bushes. Ivy-leaved toadflax grows all year in sheltered nooks in walls and often has one or two delicate mauve flowers, even during winter snows.

Left: Ivy-leaved toadflax grows throughout winter in sheltered places.

19

Hardy Insects

A peacock butterfly **(above)** may hibernate in a hollow tree among dead leaves **(below)**.

Most insects like warm weather. The warmer it is, the faster they move. The faster they move, the more difficult they are to catch. For this reason, many insects, even in summer, are only active when the Sun shines. They can fly around safely, out of reach of predators.

Many insects avoid the cold by **hibernating** during winter. Peacock butterflies and herald moths often gather in small groups in sheds and cellars where they rest without moving for as long as four or five months.

Ladybugs are even more sociable when they hibernate, and they sometimes choose the most unlikely places. Hundreds of ladybugs, all of one **species,** may congregate on an exposed tree trunk. There they experience the full blast of winter winds and may become covered with snow.

Below: Seven-spot ladybugs gather to spend winter on the trunk of an exposed thorn bush.

Below: Snow partly covers this cluster of hibernating ladybugs on the trunk of a hornbeam tree.

Left: Eight herald moths and a small tortoiseshell butterfly huddle together on the ceiling of a cellar. After hatching, the moths go right into hibernation.

Below: On a winter's night in an oak forest, a winged male winter moth mates with a wingless female.

Why they choose places like this, no one knows — but the ladybugs survive, so they must know best.

Not all adult insects become inactive in winter. Some species of moths fly only during the winter months. Male mottled umber moths and male winter moths flutter slowly under bare oak trees even while it is snowing or freezing. The males are searching for females that hatch from **pupae** on the tree trunks. The females are wingless and have to wait for the males to arrive. They produce a continuous stream of scent to attract the males.

This winter courtship takes place for a very good reason. These moths fly during winter to avoid being eaten by bats, which hibernate during the winter cold.

Cold-blooded

Top: Garden snails cluster together and seal themselves inside their shells when they hibernate.

Cold-blooded animals have bodies that are the same temperature as their surroundings. They are in danger when the weather gets extremely cold. If water in their bodies freezes, the tiny ice crystals that form cause permanent damage to their cells. This can also happen to people. Mountaineers, polar explorers, and others who become stranded in extreme cold are at risk for this condition, known as **frostbite**.

Reptiles and **amphibians** are unable to keep their bodies warm in the way that birds and mammals do. When the weather turns cold, these animals have to search for places to spend the winter where their bodies will not freeze. Newts, salamanders, and frogs that spend most of the

Right: For added protection during hibernation, garden snails choose a sheltered spot, such as underneath a log.

summer in ponds and streams climb out of the water in autumn. They crawl under logs or stones or bury themselves underground. In these places, they are insulated from the worst of the cold. They spend the winter in a state of **torpor**.

The bodies of animals contain a lot of water. Salts in the water lower its freezing point. The greater the salt level, the lower the freezing point of body fluids. A newt going into hibernation loses water in order to concentrate the salts in its blood. Its blood thickens and will not freeze easily.

Winter Flocks

Top: Starlings gather in huge flocks in winter. A single flock may contain many thousands of birds.

Many birds **migrate** to warmer climates before winter comes. For those left behind, winter brings big changes in their behaviors.

During the warmer times of the year, birds were building nests and rearing chicks. While they worked at these tasks, they stayed in one place. Each had to defend its territory against other birds of the same species. Territorial battles are forgotten when winter comes. Birds that were once enemies join together in flocks that drift from place to place, wherever food can be found.

Starlings gather in huge winter flocks. A flock sometimes contains many thousands of birds. The birds feed in fields and around houses during the day. When evening comes, they all fly to a resting place called a roost. More than a million starlings have been counted at a single roost.

Right: Brent geese gather in northern Europe in winter. They feed on grass in marshy areas close to the sea.

Some species of birds stay in one place during winter. European robins, for example, continue to defend their territories throughout the year. Even in the depths of winter, robins sing to tell their neighbors that they are in residence and will fight off any intruders. Even birds that normally flock together, such as fieldfares, become possessive when they find a good source of food. A fieldfare that finds a bush loaded with berries will fill itself up. Then it will sit in the bush and fight off any other birds that come to eat the berries.

25

White for Winter

Top: This Siberian hamster changes its brown summer coat into white for winter.

Right: A ptarmigan in winter could be mistaken for just a rounded lump of snow.

For several months each winter, much of the north is covered by a layer of snow. Some small mammals, such as voles and lemmings, spend this time underneath the snow, where they are sheltered from the worst of the weather. For them, home is similar to an igloo. Other small mammals, such as bats and dormice, find hollow trees and caves where they hibernate. There, it is safe to let their bodies become cold.

Larger animals have to move around over the snow and are at risk from predators. A brown animal atop endless white snow would be easy for a predator to see. For this reason, the arctic hare, snow lemming, and grouse-like ptarmigan shed their brown fur or feathers in autumn. They then

grow white fur or feathers for the snowy winter months. Even the predators themselves are white. This allows them to creep up on prey unseen. Arctic foxes turn white in winter, but snowy owls stay white throughout the year.

Winter in cold climates is a hard time for many animals and plants. Food is scarce or difficult to find because it is buried beneath the snow or frozen in the ground. In warmer parts of the world, winter often brings cool, rainy days that are a blessed relief from the scorching Sun of summer.

In cold climates, winter is a time when life just barely hangs on. Plants and animals prepare as best as they can to survive — until the time when the Sun's energy renews life again.

Above: An arctic hare rests in the snow in its winter white.

Below: At the end of winter, an arctic fox starts to lose its white winter coat.

Activities:

Winter Water & Snow Crystals

Winter Water

The effects of winter on plants and animals depend greatly on the changes that take place in water as it cools to below the freezing point.

Water is the essential liquid of life. If this liquid becomes solid, life can be dangerous. Most living things cannot survive continual exposure to freezing temperatures. Freezing temperatures are deadly because water expands when it turns to ice.

Not everything about water in winter is negative. The fact that water as a liquid expands rather than contracts between 39-32°F (4-0°C) is a lifesaver. This means that convection currents stop when the temperature of a pond drops below 39°F (4°C). A convection current is the one-way flow in a liquid or gas that is caused by temperature differences. As the top layer of water turns to ice, the lower layers remain safe for animals and plants to live in.

To see the effects of convection currents in water as it changes temperature, you will need some food coloring; water; a small, clear plastic jug; a large, clear plastic jug; ice cube trays; and a refrigerator with a freezer. Mix a few drops of food coloring in water in the small jug. Fill two or three compartments of an ice cube tray with the dyed water. Leave the tray in the freezer until the ice cubes are solid.

The next day, fill the large, clear jug with plain water. Leave it standing for an hour or more. Small bubbles will form on the sides of the jug from the dissolved air in the water. Tap the jug. The bubbles will rise to the surface and burst. When the water in the jug is still and bubble-free, gently place a dyed ice cube in it. Notice that the ice cube floats. Ice floats because it is less dense than water. Ice cubes often contain bubbles that make the ice float even better.

Now, it is time to watch and wait. As the ice cube melts, watch how the cold, dyed water streams down to the bottom of the jug (below). It does this because it is denser than the surrounding water. When all the ice has melted, most of the dye should be in a layer at the bottom of the jug.

The jug is like a miniature pond on a normal day. Cold, dense water is located at the bottom.

Carefully place the jug into the refrigerator so it will be in conditions similar to those at the start of winter. When winter comes, convection currents stir the pond up. The top layer cools and sinks to the bottom, pushing water from the bottom to the top. Within your jug, the dyed layer will gradually become less distinct because cold temperatures mix the water.

Snow Crystals

To make snow crystals from paper, you will need some sheets of white paper, a compass, a ruler, a pencil, and a pair of scissors (*below*). With the compass, draw a circle on a sheet of paper. Without changing the setting of the compass, mark six equally spaced points around the outside of the

circle. With the ruler and pencil, draw straight lines across the circle at these points to divide the circle into six equal pieces, like slices of pie. Then cut the circle out, turn it over, and fold it in half. There is now just half a pie, with three slices. Fold over one of the end slices so that it exactly covers the middle slice. Turn the pie over,

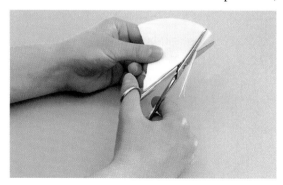

and fold the other end slice to cover the middle slice. There is now only one slice, six layers of paper thick.

You are now ready to make a snow crystal. Start by cutting away a thin strip from each side of the wedge of folded paper (*below, left*). Be careful not to cut all the edge completely away because this will result in the crystal falling apart when it is opened. Leave uncut a short piece of edge on each side near the point of the wedge.

Now you can practice your skill and artistic talent by snipping away various pieces and leaving others (*above*) to form an intricate crystal pattern.

The exciting moment in crystal making comes when you have finished snipping. Open the paper to reveal a perfect, six-sided snow crystal!

Experiment with several different patterns and sizes of paper. When you have made a pleasing collection, tape them on some colorful construction paper (*below*).

Glossary

amphibians: cold-blooded animals, such as frogs and newts, that usually have moist skin.

arid: dry.

axis: the line through the middle of an object around which the object turns.

cells: the microscopic building blocks of plant and animal bodies.

condenses: changes from vapor or steam to a liquid and sometimes a solid.

contract (v): to become smaller and occupy less space.

crystals: solids in which the molecules are arranged in a pattern, producing regular shapes with flat surfaces.

deciduous: a term to describe plants that lose their leaves during autumn.

dormant: asleep or inactive.

evergreens: plants that are in leaf all year through.

expand: to become larger and occupy more space.

frostbite: injury caused by freezing.

hemisphere: one-half of a round object, such as Earth. Earth is divided at the Equator.

hibernating: spending winter in a resting state.

hoarfrost: a thick coating of white ice crystals on top of various surfaces.

insulator: a material through which heat or electricity cannot easily pass.

latent heat: warmth required to melt a solid or vaporize a liquid.

migrate: to move from one area to another.

molecule: the smallest part of a substance, made of two or more atoms that are joined together.

plankton: tiny animals and plants that float or weakly swim in a body of water.

polar regions: areas around the ends of Earth's axis.

pupa(e): the stage in the life of an insect when it is changing from a larva into an adult.

reptiles: cold-blooded animals, such as snakes, lizards, and tortoises, that have scales.

rime: a coating of white ice.

snowflakes: ice crystals formed from condensed water vapor that attract each other.

solstice: the day on which the tilt of Earth's axis in relation to the Sun is the greatest.

species: a biologically distinct type of animal or plant that can produce offspring with another member of its specific group.

surface tension: the layer of molecules at the surface of a liquid that acts like a stretched elastic skin.

torpor: a state of deep sleep from which a living being finds it difficult to waken.

vapor: a gas formed from a liquid or solid.

Plants and Animals

The common names of plants and animals vary from language to language. Their scientific names, based on Greek or Latin words, are the same the world over. Each kind of plant or animal has two scientific names. The first name is called the genus. It starts with a capital letter. The second name is the species name. It starts with a small letter.

adder (*Vipera berus*) — Europe, Asia 23

Adélie penguin (*Pygoscelis adeliae*) — Antarctica 15

arctic fox (*Alopex lagopus*) — Arctic, Scandinavia 27

arctic hare (*Lepus arcticus*) — Arctic 27

baobab (*Adansonia gregorii*) — Australia 17

big leaf maple (*Acer macrophyllum*) — North America 10

cotoneaster (*Cotoneaster franchetii*) — Asia; introduced elsewhere 5

crucian carp (*Carassius carassius*) — Europe 14

European mole (*Talpa europaea*) — Europe, Asia 9

fieldfare (*Turdus pilaris*) — Europe 25

garden snail (*Helix aspersa*) — Europe, North Africa, Asia 22

herald moth (*Scoliopteryx libatrix*) — Europe 20, 21

holly (*Ilex aquifolium*) — Europe, western Asia; introduced to North America 17

ivy-leaved toadflax (*Gymbalaria muralis*) — southern Europe; introduced elsewhere 19

marbled newt (*Triturus marmoratus*) — southwestern Europe 23

mute swan (*Cygnus olor*) — Europe 14

nasturtium (*Tropaeolum majur*) — South America; cultivated worldwide 16

red fox (*Vulpes vulpes*) — Europe, Asia, North America; introduced to Australia 4, 5

sundew (*Drosera erythrorhiza*) — Western Australia 11

weddell seal (*Leptonychotes weddelli*) — Antarctica 15

white-tailed ptarmigan (*Lagopus leucurus*) — North America 26

winter aconite (*Eranthis hyemalis*) — Europe; introduced elsewhere 19

Books to Read

Animals in the Snow. Margaret Wise Brown (Hyperion Press)

Birds. Young Scientist Concepts and Projects (series). Jen Green (Gareth Stevens)

Butterfly Magic for Kids. Animal Magic for Kids (series). Norsgaard (Gareth Stevens)

The Cold and Hot Winter. Johanna Hurwitz (William Morrow & Company)

How Animals Protect Themselves. Animal Survival (series). Barré (Gareth Stevens)

Long Winter. Laura Ingalls Wilder (Harpercollins)

Winter: A Guide to Nature Activities and Fun. Dianne Hayley (Lone Pine)

Winter Science Projects. John Williams (Julian Messner)

Videos and Web Sites

Videos

Birds of the Backyard: Winter into Spring.
  George H. Harrison (Willow Creek)
Raging Planet: Avalanche.
  (Discover Communication)
Swiss Alpine Winter. (Education 2000)
*Symphony to America the Beautiful, Winter to
  Spring.* (Questar)
When It's Winter. (Time-Life)

Web Sites

www.worldbook.com/fun/seasons/html/
  seasons.htm
www.4seasons.org.uk/
www.southpole.com/
falcon.jmu.edu/~ramseyil/holidays.htm
backstage.nwf.org/nwf/atracks/
www.bonus.com/bonus/card/Animals_of_
  the Arctic.html

Some web sites stay current longer than others. For further web sites, use your search engines
to locate the following topics: *frost, hibernation, ice, migration, snow, solstice,* and *winter.*

Index